Speaking
Wisely

Exploring the Power of Words

POPPY SMITH

D0005575

FISHERMAN
BIBLE STUDY SERIES

Speaking Wisely

PUBLISHED BY WATERBROOK PRESS
12265 Oracle Boulevard, Suite 200
Colorado Springs, Colorado 80921
A division of Random House, Inc.

ISBN 0-87788-917-1

Printed in the United States of America
2005

10 9 8 7 6

Contents

How to Use This Studyguide

Fisherman studyguides are based on the inductive approach to Bible study. Inductive study is discovery study; we discover what the Bible says as we ask questions about its content and search for answers. This is quite different from the process in which a teacher *tells* a group *about* the Bible—what it means and what to do about it. In inductive study, God speaks directly to each of us through his Word.

A group functions best when a leader keeps the discussion on target, but the leader is neither the teacher nor the "answer person." A leader's responsibility is to *ask*—not *tell*. The answers come from the text itself as group members examine, discuss, and think together about the passage.

There are four kinds of questions in each study. The first is an *approach question*. Asked and answered before the Bible passage is read, this question breaks the ice and helps you start thinking about the topic of the Bible study. It begins to reveal where thoughts and feelings need to be transformed by Scripture.

Some of the earlier questions in each study are *observation questions*—who, what, where, when, and how—designed to help you learn some basic facts about the passage of Scripture.

Once you know what the Bible says, you need to ask, *What does it mean?* These *interpretation questions* help you discover the writer's basic message.

Next come *application questions,* which ask, *What does it mean to me?* They challenge you to live out the Scripture's life-transforming message.

Fisherman studyguides provide spaces between questions for jotting down responses as well as any related questions you would like to raise in the group. Each group member should have a copy of the studyguide and may take a turn in leading the group.

A group should use any accurate, modern translation of the Bible such as the *New International Version,* the *New American Standard Bible,* the *New Living Translation,* the *New Revised Standard Version,* the *New Jerusalem Bible,* or the *Good News Bible.* (Other translations or paraphrases of the Bible may be referred to when additional help is needed.) Bible commentaries should not be brought to a Bible study because they tend to dampen discussion and keep people from thinking for themselves.

SUGGESTIONS FOR GROUP LEADERS

1. Thoroughly read and study the Bible passage before the meeting. Get a firm grasp on its themes and begin applying its teachings for yourself. Pray that the Holy Spirit will "guide you into all truth" (John 16:13) so that your leadership will guide others.

2. If any of the studyguide's questions seem ambiguous or unnatural to you, rephrase them, feeling free to add others that seem necessary to bring out the meaning of a verse.

3. Begin (and end) the study promptly. Start by asking someone to pray that every participant will both understand the passage and be open to its transforming power. Remember, the Holy Spirit is the teacher, not you!

4. Ask for volunteers to read the passages aloud.

5. As you ask the studyguide's questions in sequence, encourage everyone to participate in the discussion. If some are silent, try gently suggesting, "Let's have an answer from someone who hasn't spoken up yet."

6. If a question comes up that you can't answer, don't be afraid to admit that you're baffled. Assign the topic as a research project for someone to report on next week, or say, "I'll do some studying and let you know what I find out."

7. Keep the discussion moving, but be sure it stays focused. Though a certain number of tangents are inevitable, you'll want to quickly bring the discussion back to the topic at hand. Also, learn to pace the discussion so that you finish the lesson in the time allotted.

8. Don't be afraid of silences; some questions take time to answer, and some people need time to gather courage to speak. If silence persists, rephrase your question, but resist the temptation to answer it yourself.

9. If someone comes up with an answer that is clearly illogical or unbiblical, ask for further clarification: "What verse suggests that to you?"

10. Discourage overuse of cross references. Learn all you can from the passage at hand, while selectively incorporating a few important references suggested in the studyguide.

11. Some questions are marked with a ✍. This indicates that further information is available in the Leader's Notes at the back of the guide.

12. For more information on getting a new Bible study group started and keeping it functioning effectively, read *You Can Start a Bible Study Group* by Gladys M. Hunt and *Pilgrims in Progress: Growing Through Groups* by Jim and Carol Plueddemann. (Both books are available from Shaw Books.)

SUGGESTIONS FOR GROUP MEMBERS

1. Learn and apply the following ground rules for effective Bible study. (If new members join the group later, review these guidelines with the whole group.)
2. Remember that your goal is to learn all that you can *from the Bible passage being studied.* Let it speak for itself without using Bible commentaries or other Bible passages. There is more than enough in each assigned passage to keep your group productively occupied for one session. Sticking to the passage saves the group from insecurity ("I don't have the right reference books—or the time to read anything else.") and confusion ("Where did *that* come from? I thought we were studying _____.").
3. Avoid the temptation to bring up those fascinating tangents that don't really grow out of the passage you are discussing. If the topic is of common interest, you can bring it up later in informal conversation after the study. Meanwhile, help one another stick to the subject.
4. Encourage one another to participate. People remember best what they discover and verbalize for

themselves. Some people are naturally shy, while others may be afraid of making a mistake. If your discussion is free and friendly and you show real interest in what other group members think and feel, the quieter ones will be more likely to speak up. Remember, the more people involved in a discussion, the richer it will be.

5. Guard yourself from answering too many questions or talking too much. Give others a chance to share their ideas. If you are one who participates easily, discipline yourself by counting to ten before you open your mouth.

6. Make personal, honest applications and commit yourself to letting God's Word change you.

Words Have Power

A few years ago, after working hard on new speaking material for a conference, I complained to one of my children, "I'm afraid I have too much to say." My highly verbal teenager responded, "Mom, you always have too much to say—about everything!" Hence, this study on the tongue comes out of my own struggle with sometimes having too much to say, especially to my husband and children.

There is no denying that words have power. Words can be inspiring, funny, and assuring. Words can also wound and destroy. Someone has said, "The tongue is more deadly than the hand because it can kill at great distances." If you've become aware of your tendency to speak before thinking of the consequences, you know how true this can be.

Words are also like windows, giving others a glimpse into your heart. Words express who you really are, what you think, and what you cherish. They reveal your joys, heartaches, attitudes, and beliefs. Based on what you say and how you say it, others can sense whether you are a safe, loving, and supportive person, someone they can trust to speak wisely to them and about them. The opposite is also true.

Relationships can quickly be ruptured and ruined by careless words. What man or woman yearns to be with a bitter, sarcastic spouse? What coworker enjoys being with a colleague who is critical and negative? What child loves to snuggle with a sharp-tongued, verbally abusive parent? What hurting believer longs for support from a cold, judgmental Christian? By God's grace, however, damaged relationships can be repaired and rebuilt by words that convey respect, forgiveness, warmth, unselfish interest, humor, and kindness.

As you work through the following biblical passages, you will find effective ways to deal with anger, negative self-talk, and gossip. You will also find helpful guidelines for using your words to encourage others, express love, and, most important, give praise to God. If you struggle with tongue-control, I pray this study will encourage you. Change is possible when we ask God for help. He can transform us into people who consistently build others up with our words.

Taming the Tongue

JAMES 1:19-21,26; 3:1-12

S ticks and stones may break my bones, but words can never hurt me." Sound familiar? As children many of us believed this little ditty but later found that it wasn't true. Harsh, mean words do hurt. They sting. They linger deep within our minds like embedded splinters. I know because, like most people, I've been on the receiving end of an untamed tongue.

Although you and I can't change what others say about us, we can hold ourselves responsible for what we say. To be honest, I have to admit that as a young Christian I sometimes used words without caring if they wounded the hearer. I didn't think about their impact or how I would feel if they were said to me. What eventually brought heart conviction and change? Reading and applying the powerful truths that James shows us in this study on taming the tongue.

1. What negative or positive words have had a lasting impact on your life?

READ JAMES 1:19-21,26.

⌇ 2. To whom was James speaking in these verses?

Why do you suppose he brought up this topic?

3. What reasons did James give for why Christians should tame their tongues (verses 20-26)?

4. What God-honoring principles for communication
    do you find in these verses?

5. Which of these principles do you find most helpful
    or most needed in your life? Why?

READ JAMES 3:1-12.

✎ 6. How did James describe the "perfect" person
       (verse 2)?

7. To what did James compare the tongue in verses
    3 through 7?

Why are these examples and metaphors effective?

8. What did James name as the source of our problems with the tongue (verse 6)?

9. What do you think James meant when he said that a person's uncontrolled tongue "sets the whole course of his life on fire" (verse 6)?

10. Review the tongue problem addressed in verses 9 through 12. Why are praising God and cursing people incompatible for Christians?

11. In what everyday circumstances might you be provoked to curse someone?

When you are tempted to react this way, what changes in your thought patterns, attitudes, or behavior would help you resist? (See also James 1:19-20.)

Life Changes

12. Generally speaking, what strengths are evident in the way you use your tongue? What weaknesses?

13. Think about the great influence your words can have for good or ill. What steps can you take to tame your tongue and be more alert to the impact your words have on others?

Choosing Wholesome Words

EPHESIANS 4:22–5:4

grew up in a non-Christian home where mild expletives were part of our everyday language. I also took secret pride in my ability to exchange sarcastic comments with others, scoring points with witty, yet cutting, remarks. It felt good to hit back or to emphatically push my viewpoint, even if I hurt another person's feelings. Then I became a Christian. My heart started to change—and so did my language.

Yet, in a world where we are continually bombarded with crude, explicit language on television, in the movies, at shopping malls, in our neighborhoods, or in the workplace, it's almost impossible, even for Christians, not to absorb what we hear. Words that make us recoil lodge in our minds and sometimes, to our shock and dismay, erupt out of our mouths. "Do not let any unwholesome talk come out of your mouths," wrote Paul (Ephesians 4:29). In a day of slipping moral standards, this study highlights the importance of choosing words that reflect who we are: followers of Christ living out *his* pure standard of thought and speech in a verbally polluted culture.

1. Describe a time, if any, when you struggled to change the way you talk. What helped you?

READ EPHESIANS 4:22-32.

2. What needs to happen before we can be motivated to change our words (verses 22-24)?

3. Why do you think Paul focused on being "made new in the attitude of your minds" before he addressed the topic of a Christian's words (verse 23)?

4. In order to change a bad habit, we must replace the behavior. Contrast the kinds of words we are to "put off" and "put on" (verses 25-32).

Put Off   *Put On*

5. Note the strong commands Paul gave in verses 25, 29, and 31. What personal lessons regarding unwholesome talk do you find in these verses?

6. What reason did Paul give for his instructions in verse 25?

Why is it important to speak truthfully with other members of the body of Christ?

🖊 7. What do you think is meant by "do not grieve the Holy Spirit of God" (verse 30)?

In what ways can we grieve God's Spirit through the words we use?

8. How do words of kindness, compassion, or forgiveness change relationships for the better (verse 32)?

If you feel comfortable doing so, describe a time when you gave or received these kinds of upbuilding words.

What impact did these words have on your Christian experience?

READ EPHESIANS 5:1-4.

9. According to verses 1 and 2, whom are we to imitate? Why?

How might knowing we are dearly loved affect what comes out of our mouths?

10. List the kinds of words that are "improper for God's holy people" (verses 3-4).

What can we do or say instead?

Life Changes

11. What steps can you take this week to imitate God through the words you choose to say to others?

12. As you consider what you've learned from this study, where do you need God's help—and the support of those in your small group—to more fully reflect who you are: a follower of Jesus?

Examining Your Self-Talk

JEREMIAH 1:1-9,17-19; ROMANS 12:1-2

We know our words can hurt and wound others, but the Bible tells us that we can also hurt and paralyze ourselves with negative self-talk. Many of us, men and women alike, struggle with self-criticism, tearing ourselves down, and minimizing our abilities. Do you find yourself saying: "God can't love me because…?" "I failed, so I'll always be a failure." "Why would anyone want to hire me, marry me, or be my friend when I'm…?" What we think about ourselves and about God can affect us emotionally, spiritually, and physically. But we're never helpless victims of our habitual thought patterns. The Bible makes it clear that we don't have to remain mired in negative and paralyzing thoughts. We can have transformed minds as we replace lies with scriptural truth.

In this study we'll see that Jeremiah, a man whom God called and used greatly, also wrestled with negative self-talk. He didn't want to do what God asked because he was sure he wouldn't succeed. However, God knew Jeremiah's potential and challenged him not to limit the impact of his life. He says the same to us.

1. When you are asked to do something that might stretch you beyond your comfort zone, what are your immediate thoughts and feelings? In what ways do these thoughts and feelings influence your response?

READ JEREMIAH 1:1-9,17-19.

2. What facts do you learn about Jeremiah from verses 1 through 3?

3. What was God's message to Jeremiah (verses 4-5)?

✐ 4. As you apply the truth of this message today, what do these verses teach you about the following:

your uniqueness

God's awareness of who you are and the potential he has put in you

5. What do you think Jeremiah meant by his reply to God (verse 6)?

Have you ever felt like Jeremiah? Explain.

6. Where was Jeremiah's focus? How did this focus affect his response to God?

7. On what could Jeremiah have focused instead (verses 8-9,19)?

What positive difference might this change of focus have made in Jeremiah's thoughts and feelings?

✎ 8. Answering Jeremiah, the Lord said, "Do not *say*, 'I am only a child.'" (verse 7, emphasis added). In what ways might saying negative words repeatedly to yourself or about yourself affect the quality of your walk with God?

How might it affect the direction of your life?

If you feel comfortable doing so, describe a time when your self-talk kept you (or almost kept you) from moving forward into a new situation.

READ ROMANS 12:1-2.

9. What did Paul urge Christians to do in verse 1?

What do you think this means for us today?

10. How might negative self-talk hinder people from presenting themselves wholeheartedly to God?

11. According to verse 2, what is the key to inner and outer transformation?

Why is this the starting place for healthy, biblical self-talk?

Life Changes

✐ 12. We must train ourselves to think the truth—about ourselves, other people, and God. What changes do you think God wants you to make in your self-talk?

13. List three steps you can take to begin renewing your mind. (See Philippians 2:12-13; 3:12-14; and 4:4-8,13 for ideas.) Share these steps with your group and help one another put them into practice.

Overcoming Anger

COLOSSIANS 3:5-14; MARK 3:1-6

H ave you ever felt so angry that you said something you never thought would come out of your mouth? Many of us probably have. Angry words are powerful: "I hate you!" "I wish you'd never been born!" "We might as well get a divorce!" "You're a complete disappointment!" Words spoken in anger pierce deep into the heart and soul. They can erode trust, produce bitterness, and turn love into resentment. If you have said or received angry words, you know their destructive and life-altering power.

The Bible has much to say about anger because it is a universal human emotion. By looking at the apostle Paul's letter to the Colossians and at Jesus' example, we'll see how God wants us to handle our anger in a way that honors rather than dishonors him.

1. Describe one thing that makes you really angry. How do you usually react?

Read Colossians 3:5-14.

2. According to verse 8, what are Christians to rid themselves of?

Define each of these terms in your own words.

3. List all the reasons you can think of for why we are to rid ourselves of angry and hateful words.

4. Read Ephesians 4:26-27. What gives the devil a foothold in our lives? Why?

5. What effect does anger have on your words and how you say them?

    How do angry words affect our relationships?

6. God never asks anything of us that is impossible.
    With this in mind, what encouragement and hope
    for change do you find in Colossians 3:8-10?

READ MARK 3:1-6.

7. Describe the situation Jesus encountered in this
    passage.

8. What emotions was he experiencing? What
    prompted them?

9. Think about ways people commonly express their
    anger. What did Jesus not do even though he was
    angry?

    What did he do instead?

✍ 10. What helpful lessons for overcoming anger do you find from Jesus' example?

11. What further wisdom for handling anger-provoking situations do you find in the following passages?

Proverbs 10:19

Proverbs 12:16

Proverbs 13:3

Life Changes

12. If you are comfortable doing so, describe a situation
     you are currently facing in which you realize that
     you need to control your words and change the
     way you handle your anger.

13. List at least one person you can ask to pray for you
     and hold you accountable.

Speaking Words of Love in Your Family

I SAMUEL 1:1-8,19-23; 16:1-13; 17:25-30

M y friend Judy grew up in a warm and loving family where she was emotionally nourished with encouraging and affirming words of approval. Another friend, Dottie, received constant criticism and blame for merely existing. As a result of the words spoken in each family, who do you think is a warm and affirming adult, and who do you think struggles with feeling that she has any value?

"Sometimes we aren't as careful about what we say to our spouse as we are to others," confessed a young, newly married friend. This is also true of words spoken by parents to children, sibling to sibling, and one close family member to another. Whether we are married or single, we don't always find family to be the emotionally safe and nurturing place God designed it to be. Because the words we use within our families have long-lasting influence for good or evil, let's see what two families in the Old Testament teach us about the importance of speaking words of love to family members.

1. Think back to how members in your family of origin communicated with one another. In what ways has this influenced how you communicate with your spouse or family members?

READ 1 SAMUEL 1:1-8,19-23.

↗ 2. What do you learn about Elkanah from this passage?

↗ 3. Compare and contrast Peninnah's and Hannah's personalities and circumstances.

4. What words might Peninnah have used to provoke and irritate Hannah (verses 6-7)?

What effect did Peninnah's treatment have on Hannah (verse 8)?

5. How did Elkanah respond to Hannah's emotional pain?

What effect might his words in verses 8 and 23 have had on their relationship?

6. Both men and women struggle with emotionally stressful circumstances. What help do you find in Hannah and Elkanah's story for supporting your spouse or another family member who is going through a difficult time?

READ 1 SAMUEL 16:1-13; 17:25-30.

7. How was David treated by his father when Samuel came to anoint God's choice for king (16:10-11)?

8. How did David's oldest brother respond when David asked about Goliath (17:28)?

9. What seemed to be the attitudes toward David in these two family incidents?

What long-term effects do you think rejection and put-downs like these can have on a young person?

10. Read Psalm 18:1-3, one of the many psalms David wrote. How do you think David's relationship with God helped him overcome the negative effects of his family environment?

What personal encouragement do you find in these verses?

✐ 11. Proverbs 10:21 says, "The lips of the righteous nourish many." The following acrostic BEST suggests ways we can nourish and encourage others:

BLESS with your words. Be kind, affirming, and gracious.

EDIFY your loved ones; build them up. Show an interest in their lives. Ask what they are doing, how God is blessing them, what God is doing in their lives.

SHARE your feelings with others in an open, calm, honest, and relaxed manner. Give others permission to do the same.

TOUCH others (in an appropriate manner) when you talk to them to show them that you care.

What do you learn from this acrostic about how to verbally love and nourish your child, spouse, or other family member?

Which of these areas come easily for you? In which areas do you want to improve?

Life Changes

12. Describe a real-life situation in which speaking words of love could make a difference in your family.

13. Write down the names of your immediate family members and ask yourself, "What nourishing words do they need to hear from me at this time?" Jot down how you can BEST speak to them and when you will do this.

Getting a Grip on Gossip

NEHEMIAH 6:1-14; PROVERBS 12:13-23

The owner of a British newspaper notorious for its gossip once proudly declared, "There's money in muck!" In America, too, various television programs and magazines specialize in digging up whatever juicy tidbits they can find about the rich and famous. Innocent information about families, homes, hobbies, or lifestyle isn't enough. What the public wants is private, preferably titillating information—in other words, gossip.

Unfortunately, some Christians are not immune to craving gossip either, even though gossip shreds relationships and reputations, causes pain and anguish, and greatly harms the work of God in individual Christians and churches. Ancient times were no different from today, however, as we will see in this study of Nehemiah, a leader of Israel, who also dealt with malicious gossip.

1. In your opinion, when is talking about someone else "gossip" and when is it not?

READ NEHEMIAH 6:1-14.

✍ 2. Nehemiah was a godly leader who was involved personally in rebuilding the city wall of Jerusalem. Summarize in your own words the many ways Nehemiah's enemies tried to discredit and demoralize him.

✍ 3. Why did Nehemiah's enemies attack him (verses 2,9,13)?

4. List the ways Nehemiah responded to each assault on his character (verses 2-4,8-9,11-13; see also 4:8-9).

5. Why do you think Nehemiah was able to persevere and not be overcome by the lies and gossip spread about him?

6. What motivates people to gossip, slander, or misrepresent another person?

If you are comfortable doing so—and without giving names—share an example of a time when you were the object of gossip. How did it affect you? How did you handle it?

7. What helpful lessons do you learn from the way Nehemiah handled his difficult situation?

Read Proverbs 12:13-23.

8. In what ways does verse 13—"An evil man is trapped by his sinful talk"—apply to a gossip?

9. List the phrases in this passage that describe the person who uses his or her tongue wisely.

   Which of these descriptions would you like to be said of you? Why?

10. What further insights for getting a grip on gossip do you find in the following verses?

    Matthew 5:44

    Matthew 18:15

    Philippians 2:3-4

In what ways can taking these steps help contain the damage gossip does to us and to others?

Life Changes

11. Gossip doesn't just take place at work or during get-togethers with friends. It can frequently come in the guise of a prayer request, cloaked with expressions of concern. Parents can gossip about others, not realizing that their children are absorbing every word. Family gatherings can degenerate into information-sharing sessions where a juicy tidbit gets passed on to many others. Where or with whom do you find it most difficult to resist joining in on gossip? Explain.

12. In light of gossip's great power to hurt innocent people, what can you do to be known by colleagues, fellow believers, friends, and family as a person whose tongue "brings healing" and not harm (Proverbs 12:18)?

Encouraging Others

ACTS 4:32-37; 9:26-28; 11:22-26

One night during a particularly low time in my life, I lay on my bed crying and asking God if he knew or cared about the situation that was overwhelming me. Within minutes the phone rang. A friend from the other side of the country, who had never called me before, asked how I was. She had felt led to call right then, not knowing how down I was. Her encouraging words meant far more to me than a mere long-distance phone call from a friend. They reassured me that God did indeed know and care about what was happening in my life.

Everyone needs encouragement—and some of us need it more than others! Encouragement cheers us on, gives us hope, inspires confidence, and renews our strength in difficult circumstances. This study shows us that encouraging and supporting others through our words is a privilege, and the responsibility of every Christian.

1.   What words have encouraged you recently? What
     made them special?

Read Acts 4:32-37.

2.   What attitudes and actions characterized the early
     church in Jerusalem?

⌐3. What do you learn about Barnabas (Joseph) from
     this passage?

Read Acts 9:26-28.

4.   What role did Barnabas play in Saul's (Paul's) life
     when he first went to Jerusalem?

5. In what ways do you think Barnabas encouraged Paul?

How did it further God's purposes for Paul's life?

READ ACTS 11:22-26.

⚘ 6. List the details described in this passage about the church at Antioch. (See also 11:19-21.)

7. Why do you think the church at Jerusalem chose Barnabas to go to Antioch (verses 22-24)?

8. What did Barnabas encourage the new believers in Antioch to do (verses 23)?

ℐ 9. What words would you use to encourage someone to remain true to the Lord in spite of difficult circumstances?

ℐ 10. After Barnabas saw the need in Antioch, he sought out Saul's help (verses 25-26). In what ways do you think Saul (Paul) benefited from spending a year with a man like Barnabas?

Life Changes

11. Who has been a Barnabas in your life? What words has he or she used that have been an encouragement to you?

12. Brainstorm practical ways in which you can offer words of encouragement to others (write an encouraging note, make a phone call, affirm a person's character, give a gentle prod, etc.). Which of these will you choose to do this week? For whom?

Glorifying God

PSALM 103

A s a new Christian I would often drive to work singing praise songs as loud as I could. Overwhelmed with gratitude and love, I wept, tears streaking my cheeks with mascara; but I didn't care. Knowing that the Creator, the Eternal One who holds all things together, had given his Son for me amazed and thrilled me to the core of my being. Everything in me longed to give him praise. Years later I still find that praising God changes my perspective and fills me with hope and joy.

"Praise the Lord, O my soul." "Sing to him, sing praise to him. Glory in his holy name." "Give thanks to the Lord, for he is good; his love endures forever." With these and many other phrases, David's love for God flows through the psalms. In this last study on the power of words, David directs our hearts to the greatness of God and draws us to the highest possible use of language: praise and worship.

1. What thrills you most about your relationship with God?

⌀ READ PSALM 103.

2. What did David tell himself to do (verses 1-2)?

    Why do you think he would talk to himself like this?

3. List the benefits of life with God that David recounted (verses 3-5).

4. How did David describe God's character in verses 7 and 8?

5. What further understanding of God do you gain from verses 10 through 12?

In what ways is your understanding of God similar to or different from the descriptions of him in this passage?

6. What effect does remembering God's character and blessings have on your worship?

7. What reason did David give for the Lord's compassion (verses 13-14)?

How does God's understanding affect his dealings with us?

8. What phrase is repeated in verses 11, 13, and 17?

Why do you think it is necessary first to "fear" (reverence) God before you can know him as a loving, compassionate Father?

9. Observe the contrasts between God and human beings given in verses 15 through 19. In what ways do these show the greatness of God?

10. List your own words of praise from reading this psalm on the character of God.

Life Changes

11. David's adoration and praise for God flowed out of his whole being. He wrote psalms, sang, prayed, and danced in worship. What steps can you take to make adoration and praise a regular part of your walk with God?

12. Take a few minutes to look back through this entire studyguide, reflecting on all you have learned. Which lesson on the power of words has made the greatest impact on you? What differences are you seeing in your life and in how you speak, as a result?

Leader's Notes

STUDY 1: TAMING THE TONGUE

Question 2. It has been believed, since at least the third century, that the author of this book is James, the brother of Jesus. James probably wrote his letter to Jewish believers between A.D. 45–50. These early Christians had fled Jerusalem after persecution had erupted following the killing of Stephen, which left them without direct contact with the apostles. Reports of their difficulties and struggles reached James in Jerusalem, and he responded as their pastor, urging them to make needed changes in both their personal lives and corporate relationships (Adapted from Kenneth L. Barker and John R. Kohlengerger III, *NIV Bible Commentary,* Grand Rapids: Zondervan, 1994, pp. 1016-17).

Question 6. The New Testament use of the word *perfect,* found in James 3:2, means "spiritually mature."

Question 8. "The tongue's wickedness has its source in hell itself.... Satan uses the tongue to divide people and pit them against one another" (*Life Application Bible,* Wheaton, Ill.: Tyndale, 1991, p. 2249).

Question 10. In James's day, cursing another person meant you wished some sort of evil would befall them. In Bible times, as is true in some cultures today, a curse was believed to possess the power to inflict evil on the recipient.

Study 2: Choosing Wholesome Words

Question 6. Unity is a major theme of Ephesians 4. Christians are called to "make every effort to keep the unity of the Spirit" because we share "one body and one Spirit...one Lord, one faith, one baptism; one God and Father of all" (Ephesians 4:3-6). In this passage Paul reminds the Ephesians again that they are members of one body; therefore, lying or falsehood of any kind has no place in the Christian community.

Question 7. The Holy Spirit is not a vague force; he is a person, fully divine, one with the Father and Son. He has intelligence, will, and emotions, traditionally regarded as the three fundamental elements of personhood. As a person, he can be grieved, quenched, and resisted. Jesus always spoke of the Holy Spirit as a person (see John 16:8), just as Paul did in Romans 8:26. Believers are sealed (marked) with the Holy Spirit at salvation as a guarantee of ultimate redemption. (See Ephesians 1:13-14.)

Question 10. Encourage one anther by asking members to relate how they handle the temptation to "blend in" by using similar language in peer-pressure situations.

Study 3: Examining Your Self-Talk

Question 2. After Isaiah, Jeremiah is considered the second of the major prophets of the Old Testament. God called him as a youth to warn the people of coming judgment if they did not abandon their idolatry. His ministry extended over the last tragic forty years of the kingdom of Judah to the destruction of Jerusalem and the deportation of its inhabitants to

Babylon. Jeremiah's sermons were intensely opposed, and he suffered a great deal, yet he remained faithful to God's call on his life.

Question 4. For further study on our worth to God, see Psalm 139:13-16 and Ephesians 2:10.

Question 8. Telling yourself things that aren't true not only hinders your awareness of God's unconditional love and acceptance, but it can also keep you from becoming who God wants you to be and doing all he has planned for your life. Negative self-talk can cripple your walk with God. Positive self-talk, taken from Scripture, helps you soar in your relationship with him.

Question 9. Christians do not live a life of sacrifice in order to obtain God's mercy; rather, we are called to live for God as a *response* to his mercy expressed in the cross of Christ. Paul's reference to sacrifice points to the Old Testament offerings in which the whole burnt offering ascended to God and could never be reclaimed. It belonged to God. Offering ourselves as living sacrifices has in view a day-by-day life of loving service to God (Adapted from the *NIV Bible Commentary,* p. 582).

Question 12. To begin this process, ask the Holy Spirit to help you question any automatic, negative assumptions that come to mind. Make a practice of challenging defeatist and discouraging thoughts. Replace these thoughts with accurate statements based on facts, not feelings, and with scriptural verses of truth (Adapted from Poppy Smith, *I Wish I Could Be More...,* Minneapolis: Bethany House, 1999, pp. 102, 106).

STUDY 4: OVERCOMING ANGER

Question 2. "Paul reminded his readers in Colossians 3:1-4 of their union with Christ and the power and encouragement that gives for a changed life.… We are charged to 'put to death' (lit., to make dead) the old life in everyday practice. This verb suggests we are not to excuse or tolerate evil acts or attitudes; rather, we are to wipe them out, to rid ourselves of them like stripping off filthy garments. *Anger* means the settled feeling of intense displeasure or antagonism and the passionate outburst of that feeling. *Malice* denotes a vicious disposition that prompts one to injure one's neighbor. *Slander* is making insulting and false statements about others. *Filthy language* may denote cursing or abusive speech" (*NIV Bible Commentary*, pp. 834-35).

Question 8. While fully God (Colossians 2:9), Jesus was also fully human, experiencing the full gamut of appropriate emotions; yet he never sinned (Hebrews 4:15). The apostle Paul clearly stated that anger is not necessarily a sin: "In your anger do not sin" (Ephesians 4:26). Jesus' anger was an appropriate expression of his holy and righteous indignation against the Pharisees' sin of indifference and lack of love.

Question 10. See also James 1:19-20 and Galatians 5:16,22-23.

STUDY 5: SPEAKING WORDS OF LOVE IN YOUR FAMILY

Question 2. Polygamy was commonly practiced in ancient times, even among the Hebrew people. But many Hebrew men had only one wife, perhaps due to the expense of supporting more than one family.

Question 3. Among Jewish women there was great honor in bearing children. The promise of the Messiah coming out of Israel caused every Hebrew woman to long for a son, hoping that he might be the Promised One. Because of these and other blessings pronounced on childbearing women, Hannah's barrenness was considered a stigma and a curse.

Question 11. For further practical ways to nourish one another at home, it may be helpful to look at Colossians 3:12-14.

Study 6: Getting a Grip on Gossip

Question 2. After living in captivity under the Babylonians for many years, thousands of Jews returned to their land under Zerubbabel and Ezra (536–457 B.C.). Ninety years after the first return, Nehemiah heard that the walls and gates of Jerusalem were still in great disrepair. Following much anguished prayer, Nehemiah asked the king of Persia for permission to return to Jerusalem to restore the city of his fathers. Nehemiah led the third major return to Jerusalem in 445 B.C. Sanballat was the governor of Samaria, and Tobiah was probably another governor under the Persians.

Question 3. According to Nehemiah 4:1-3, Sanballat was angry that the Jews were rebuilding the wall. He opposed Nehemiah from the beginning, perhaps seeing him as a rival for power in the area.

Question 6. People gossip for many reasons: to feel important, to gain attention or power, to feel like an insider, to get even, to seek favors, or because they feel superior to others. Proverbs 15:28 makes it clear how we should respond to the temptation to gossip: "The heart of the righteous weighs its answers, but the mouth of the wicked gushes evil."

STUDY 7: ENCOURAGING OTHERS

Question 3. Barnabas "was a Levite by birth, a member of the Jewish tribe that carried out temple duties. But his family had moved to Cyprus, so Barnabas didn't serve in the temple" (*Life Application Bible,* p. 1952).

Question 6. Antioch was a city about three hundred miles north of Jerusalem. Some of the early Christians who fled Jerusalem after the martyrdom of Stephen settled in Antioch, where they were first called Christians. At first the early Christians only shared their faith with fellow Jews. After some of them preached to Greeks (a term for non-Jews), however, the Antioch church thrived. It was from Antioch that Paul began his first missionary journey and where he fought on behalf of Gentile believers for freedom from Jewish laws.

Question 9. You may want to look at passages such as Hebrews 10:23-25 and Colossians 1:9-13 for specific words of hope, comfort, and encouragement to say to others.

Question 10. Paul became the ultimate example of using words to spur others on. He encouraged, comforted, and urged the Thessalonians to live lives worthy of God (1 Thessalonians

2:12). In writing to the Romans, he stressed that there is no condemnation to those who are in Christ Jesus (8:1)—a strong word of encouragement, both then and now, to those who feel condemned when they fail in some way. Paul's epistles, while dealing with many difficult issues, nevertheless overflow with encouraging words for Christians of every age and culture.

STUDY 8: GLORIFYING GOD

Read Psalm 103. The psalms are a collection of writings that formed the national hymnbook of ancient Israel. A collection of religious poems, they tell of God's greatness, his loving-kindness, his righteous judgment, and his heart of compassion for those who love him. David wrote many, but not all, of the psalms, and it is through his heartfelt words that we learn to be transparent before God, bringing him our every need.

Question 6. "Worship focuses on God's matchless worth—adoring him, magnifying his name, and giving him the glory he desires and deserves.... Worship is the creature's response of love to the Creator, the child's delight in her Father. The once shame-filled person's amazement at the mercy and forgiveness of a perfect God.... In his wisdom, God has created us in such a way that as worship becomes part of our spiritual walk, we benefit. By focusing on his greatness and perfection our ability to trust deepens. We also reap a spiritual vitality that permeates our lives with joy and peace" (Poppy Smith, *Keep Growing,* Minneapolis: Bethany House, 2001, p. 91).

What Should We Study Next?

I f you enjoyed this Fisherman Bible Studyguide, you might want to explore our full line of Fisherman Resources and Bible Studyguides. The following books offer time-tested Fisherman inductive Bible studies for individuals or groups.

FISHERMAN RESOURCES

The Art of Spiritual Listening: Responding to God's Voice Amid the Noise of Life by Alice Fryling
Balm in Gilead by Dudley Delffs
The Essential Bible Guide by Whitney T. Kuniholm
Questions from the God Who Needs No Answers: What Is He Really Asking of You? by Carolyn and Craig Williford
Reckless Faith: Living Passionately as Imperfect Christians by Jo Kadlecek
Soul Strength: Spiritual Courage for the Battles of Life by Pam Lau

FISHERMAN BIBLE STUDYGUIDES

Topical Studies
Angels by Vinita Hampton Wright
Becoming Women of Purpose by Ruth Haley Barton
Building Your House on the Lord: A Firm Foundation for Family Life (Revised Edition) by Steve and Dee Brestin

Discipleship: The Growing Christian's Lifestyle by James and
Martha Reapsome

*Doing Justice, Showing Mercy: Christian Action in Today's
World* by Vinita Hampton Wright

Encouraging Others: Biblical Models for Caring by Lin
Johnson

The End Times: Discovering What the Bible Says by
E. Michael Rusten

Examining the Claims of Jesus by Dee Brestin

Friendship: Portraits in God's Family Album by Steve and
Dee Brestin

The Fruit of the Spirit: Growing in Christian Character by
Stuart Briscoe

Great Doctrines of the Bible by Stephen Board

Great Passages of the Bible by Carol Plueddemann

Great Prayers of the Bible by Carol Plueddemann

Growing Through Life's Challenges by James and Martha
Reapsome

Guidance & God's Will by Tom and Joan Stark

Heart Renewal: Finding Spiritual Refreshment by Ruth
Goring

Higher Ground: Steps Toward Christian Maturity by Steve
and Dee Brestin

*Images of Redemption: God's Unfolding Plan Through the
Bible* by Ruth E. Van Reken

Integrity: Character from the Inside Out by Ted W.
Engstrom and Robert C. Larson

Lifestyle Priorities by John White

Marriage: Learning from Couples in Scripture by R. Paul
and Gail Stevens

Miracles by Robbie Castleman

One Body, One Spirit: Building Relationships in the Church
by Dale and Sandy Larsen

The Parables of Jesus by Gladys Hunt

Parenting with Purpose and Grace by Alice Fryling

Prayer: Discovering What Scripture Says by Timothy Jones
and Jill Zook-Jones

The Prophets: God's Truth Tellers by Vinita Hampton Wright

Proverbs and Parables: God's Wisdom for Living by Dee
Brestin

Satisfying Work: Christian Living from Nine to Five by
R. Paul Stevens and Gerry Schoberg

Senior Saints: Growing Older in God's Family by James and
Martha Reapsome

The Sermon on the Mount: The God Who Understands Me
by Gladys M. Hunt

Speaking Wisely: Exploring the Power of Words by Poppy
Smith

Spiritual Disciplines: The Tasks of a Joyful Life by Larry
Sibley

Spiritual Gifts by Karen Dockrey

Spiritual Hunger: Filling Your Deepest Longings by Jim and
Carol Plueddemann

A Spiritual Legacy: Faith for the Next Generation by Chuck
and Winnie Christensen

Spiritual Warfare by A. Scott Moreau

The Ten Commandments: God's Rules for Living by Stuart
Briscoe

Ultimate Hope for Changing Times by Dale and Sandy
Larsen

When Faith Is All You Have: A Study of Hebrews 11 by
Ruth E. Van Reken

Where Your Treasure Is: What the Bible Says About Money
 by James and Martha Reapsome
Who Is God? by David P. Seemuth
Who Is Jesus? In His Own Words by Ruth E. Van Reken
Who Is the Holy Spirit? by Barbara H. Knuckles and Ruth
 E. Van Reken
Wisdom for Today's Woman: Insights from Esther by Poppy
 Smith
Witnesses to All the World: God's Heart for the Nations by
 Jim and Carol Plueddemann
Women at Midlife: Embracing the Challenges by Jeanie
 Miley
Worship: Discovering What Scripture Says by Larry Sibley

Bible Book Studies

Genesis: Walking with God by Margaret Fromer and
 Sharrel Keyes
Exodus: God Our Deliverer by Dale and Sandy Larsen
Ruth: Relationships That Bring Life by Ruth Haley
 Barton
Ezra and Nehemiah: A Time to Rebuild by James
 Reapsome
(For Esther, see Topical Studies, *Wisdom for Today's
 Woman*)
Job: Trusting Through Trials by Ron Klug
Psalms: A Guide to Prayer and Praise by Ron Klug
Proverbs: Wisdom That Works by Vinita Hampton Wright
Ecclesiastes: A Time for Everything by Stephen Board
Song of Songs: A Dialogue of Intimacy by James Reapsome
Jeremiah: The Man and His Message by James Reapsome

Jonah, Habakkuk, and Malachi: Living Responsibly by
   Margaret Fromer and Sharrel Keyes
Matthew: People of the Kingdom by Larry Sibley
Mark: God in Action by Chuck and Winnie Christensen
Luke: Following Jesus by Sharrel Keyes
John: The Living Word by Whitney Kuniholm
Acts 1–12: God Moves in the Early Church by Chuck and
   Winnie Christensen
Acts 13–28, see *Paul* under Character Studies
Romans: The Christian Story by James Reapsome
1 Corinthians: Problems and Solutions in a Growing Church
   by Charles and Ann Hummel
Strengthened to Serve: 2 Corinthians by Jim and Carol
   Plueddemann
Galatians, Titus, and Philemon: Freedom in Christ by
   Whitney Kuniholm
Ephesians: Living in God's Household by Robert Baylis
Philippians: God's Guide to Joy by Ron Klug
Colossians: Focus on Christ by Luci Shaw
Letters to the Thessalonians by Margaret Fromer and Sharrel
   Keyes
Letters to Timothy: Discipleship in Action by Margaret
   Fromer and Sharrel Keyes
Hebrews: Foundations for Faith by Gladys Hunt
James: Faith in Action by Chuck and Winnie Christensen
1 and 2 Peter, Jude: Called for a Purpose by Steve and Dee
   Brestin
1, 2, 3 John: How Should a Christian Live? by Dee
   Brestin
Revelation: The Lamb Who Is the Lion by Gladys Hunt

Bible Character Studies

Abraham: Model of Faith by James Reapsome

David: Man After God's Own Heart by Robbie Castleman

Elijah: Obedience in a Threatening World by Robbie
Castleman

Great People of the Bible by Carol Plueddemann

King David: Trusting God for a Lifetime by Robbie
Castleman

Men Like Us: Ordinary Men, Extraordinary God by Paul
Heidebrecht and Ted Scheuermann

Moses: Encountering God by Greg Asimakoupoulos

Paul: Thirteenth Apostle (Acts 13–28) by Chuck and
Winnie Christensen

Women Like Us: Wisdom for Today's Issues by Ruth Haley
Barton

Women Who Achieved for God by Winnie Christensen

Women Who Believed God by Winnie Christensen